BOWIE

A to Z

Smith Street Books

INTRODUCTION

When David Bowie died on January 16, 2016, what followed was the public outpouring of grief that usually accompanies the passing of a rock star. But there was something very different this time. While someone who may have been choked up by Lemmy from Motorhead's death a month earlier might not have been phased when The Specials drummer John Bradbury died on the same day, and they might not have had more than a passing interest at Blitz Kid Steve Strange's untimely demise in February 2015. However, when Bowie died, this expression of grief wasn't just coming from a group of die-hard fans or obsessives. It wasn't just the music critics or the aficionados trying hard to articulate their feelings. The accolades, tears and a very real sense of loss was seemingly coming from everywhere: from people from many different walks of life and many different corners of the world.

It stands as a moving testament to the true impact of Bowie's artistic legacy and the jaw-dropping breadth of his influence. Just as he moved through the phases of his own life, Bowie had been the soundtrack to the phases of the lives of so many others – growing with them, anticipating them, changing them. If you were into rock and roll, a social misfit, LGBTI, theatrical, quirky, or just liked a great tune, Bowie had been there, speaking to you, comforting you, making you feel like you weren't alone.

He once said, 'Tomorrow belongs to those who can hear it coming'. From hippy folk to glam, plastic soul to new wave, all the way to industrial and drum and bass, Bowie possessed an uncanny ability to pinpoint and absorb the now and translate it into music that not only spoke of the times but moved them forward as well – while still staking a claim in the upper reaches of the charts. He defied categorisation. Sometimes he described himself as a visiting alien, other times as an ordinary man who wanted to rise above. In every way, Bowie embodied his art – elevating him from rock star to icon. Music was his vessel, his way of achieving immortality and his lasting legacy. But enough words. As Bowie said, 'Talking about art is like dancing about architecture'.

STEVE WIDE

A
is also for

'Ashes to Ashes'

A classic tune from *Scary Monsters (and Super Creeps)*, and the dark return of 'Space Oddity's' astronaut Major Tom. The iconic video was directed by Bowie and David Mallet and was, at the time, the most expensive film clip ever made (with a budget of £250 000). The video featured Bowie in his famous Pierrot costume, as well as a cameo from Steve Strange.

...

Arnold Corns

A band started by Bowie in 1971, said to be inspired by the Pink Floyd song 'Arnold Layne'. The side-project was a kind of lead-up to Ziggy Stardust.

...

Absolute Beginners

A British rock musical-turned-film directed by Julian Temple and featuring David Bowie alongside Sade and Patsy Kensit. The movie was a massive flop at the box office, but Bowie's (passable) recording of the title track still reached number two in the UK charts.

...

Androgyny

Almost as famous as his contribution to music is Bowie's unconventional and progressive approach to gender presentation. From early in his career Bowie favoured boundary-pushing androgynous looks, blending elements of male and female fashion and of course, wearing tons of make-up.

Lady Gaga got an Aladdin Sane tattoo on her left side before her Bowie tribute appearance at the 2016 Grammys.

Mike Garson's piano on the title track was improvised and recorded in one take.

The album's title track used to give Bowie's son Duncan nightmares.

An original title for the album was *Love Aladdin Vein* but was dropped due to the drug use implications.

The single 'Drive in Saturday' is about a future where people have to go to the drive-in to relearn sex by watching old movies.

Bowie came up with the idea of the lightning bolt, but the teardrop was added by photographer Brian Duffy.

Bowie told his friends that the 'A Lad Insane' wordplay was inspired by his brother who was diagnosed with schizophrenia.

LOVE ALADDIN VEIN

Lulu covered 'Watch The Man' on the B-side of her version of another Bowie song 'The Man Who Sold the World'. Both tracks were produced by Bowie and Mick Ronson.

American soul singer Claudia Lennear was said to be the inspiration for 'Lady Grinning Soul' (and incidentally also for the Rolling Stones' 'Brown Sugar').

The album went to number 17 in America making it Bowie's most successful album there to date.

A is for ALADDIN SANE

Released in April 1973, the album cover art for *Aladdin Sane* features what is perhaps Bowie's most enduring and recognisable image: his stark face cut through by that iconic lightning bolt. The bolt divides Bowie in schizophrenic fashion and the album title's clever wordplay was intended to show the two states of Bowie's mind at the time: he wanted to be the performer, but was worn down from touring and cash-poor from mixed reactions throughout America. Yet, he was invigorated by the States and its influences, so while 'A Lad Insane' teetered on the edge of collapse, 'Aladdin Sane' was the magical Jean Genie who emerged from within the imprisoning lamp that was Ziggy Stardust, to show the world a new Bowie. It made sense to make Ziggy part two, but Bowie also wanted to break away. Cleverly, he invented a character more appealing to America, and introduced Bowie the innovator and Bowie the changeling to the world by eschewing Ziggy's glam boogie stompers for a more stripped-down rock and roots approach. The title track featuring avant-guard jazz pianist Mike Garson was a revelation, and although the album didn't come close to the musical heights of *Ziggy* it went to number one in the UK and gave Bowie the belief he needed to embark on constant reinvention.

B is for BERLIN

The Berlin Trilogy of *Low*, *Heroes* and *Lodger* were recorded between '77 and '78, and are regarded as a pinnacle of Bowie's creativity, and yet another stylistic turning point. Bowie moved to Berlin to escape America and the cocaine-fuelled excesses that had followed the success of 'Fame' and 'Golden Years'. Berlin was the antithesis of America – the wall was still up and Bowie was relatively unknown in the city – and Bowie took up residence in Schöneberg, one of the city's bleakest areas. He was joined there by Iggy Pop, who also needed a sabbatical, and Brian Eno and Tony Visconti were brought over to produce and engineer respectively. Eno's influence is all over *Low* and *Heroes* – synthesiser washes, ambient soundtracks and odd distant noises were sculpted straight out of Berlin's urban post-war landscape. The songs are classic new wave and post-punk, born from the pioneering work of Krautrock artists like Can and Kraftwerk – yet they predicted what was to come once punk had collapsed into a pool of its own vomit. Though one of his least commercially successful times, Berlin provided Bowie with a new direction, allowing him to create some of the most influential music of his career.

Bowie became estranged from Angie during this time and she kept his son Duncan away from him.

Bowie's personal assistant Coco Schwab is credited with 'stabilising' Bowie in Berlin by turning his apartment into a makeshift gallery and taking him to art exhibitions. He left her two million dollars in his will.

Bowie described his three Berlin albums, and especially the song 'Heroes', as 'his DNA'.

Low was made while Bowie was withdrawing from his addiction to cocaine. The title clearly refers to his emotional state during the comedown, but also maintains a clever visual pun, with the side-on photograph of Bowie alluding to his current 'low profile'.

In keeping with his 'anonymity', Bowie adopted workers' clothes while living in Berlin.

Bowie, Iggy Pop and Lou Reed often hit the clubs at night, especially Dschungel, Berlin's answer to Studio 54.

Writer Rory MacLean reported that he and Iggy Pop were once in a car with Bowie, who was driving around a hotel car park screaming that he wanted to 'end it all'.

Eno said that while recording, Bowie didn't eat. He would get home at six in the morning and crack a raw egg into his mouth.

All three LPs were recorded at the Hansa Tonstudio in Kreuzberg. Built in 1974, it was often referred to as 'Hansa by the wall'.

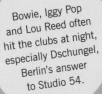

Bowie said that, despite leaving the cocaine capital of the world, Los Angeles, for the smack capital of the world, Berlin, he felt much safer there since heroin held no appeal for him.

B

is also for

Blackstar
Bowie's 25th studio LP and the last to be released during his lifetime, *Blackstar* was described by Visconti as Bowie's 'parting gift' to his fans. It was his only LP to reach number one in America and only one of three albums to not feature Bowie's image on the cover.

...

'Boys Keep Swinging'
Although he was accused of sexism, Bowie said 'Boy's Keep Swinging', 'played on the idea of the colonisation of gender'. It went to number seven in the UK, Bowie's first chart hit since 'Sound and Vision' two years earlier.

...

Bowie Bonds
Bowie offered investors shares in future royalties from 25 albums for ten years. He was able to use the proceeds of this financial innovation to buy back the rights to his early recordings.

...

BowieNet
Bowie launched his own internet service provider in '98. While the benefits of controlling his output were clear, Bowie also saw the potential in the internet's broader-reaching uses, saying at the time, 'If I was 19 again, I'd bypass music and go right to the internet.'

...

Boy George
Boy George stated after Bowie's death, 'I look this way because of Bowie. Bowie's look wasn't camp. That's what people often get wrong. He looked alien, he looked 'other', but he wasn't beautiful. Even when he wore make-up and white knee-high boots he looked like a man.'

C

is also for

China Girl
Written for Iggy Pop's LP *The Idiot*, Bowie recorded a more chart-friendly version for *Let's Dance*. The video's star was New Zealand actress and model Geeling Ng. Bowie struck up a relationship with her in Sydney and she travelled to Europe with him on the 'Serious Moonlight' tour.

...

Cocaine spoon
Now a fixture in the touring *Bowie Is* exhibition; Bowie wore a small cocaine spoon around his neck during the recording of *Station to Station*. He was a regular user by that stage.

...

Collaborator
Bowie's career was replete with iconic collaborations. From the stunning 'Under Pressure' with Queen, to Iggy Pop's *The Idiot*; the 'we don't hate each other at all' recording of 'Dancing in the Street' with Mick Jagger, the sublime *Transformer* with Lou Reed and 'Fame' with John Lennon; plus recordings with Bing Crosby, Cher, Luther Vandross, Tina Turner, Trent Reznor, Massive Attack and Arcade Fire, just to name a few (and those are just the musical collaborations). His work with Brian Eno is some of his best, and producer Tony Visconti was a regular fixture.

...

Carinda
A town in the far north of New South Wales, Australia, where Bowie's famous 'Let's Dance' video was filmed, with iconic scenes shot in the Carinda Hotel. The young couple in the video were played by Joelene King and Terry Roberts, students of the Aboriginal Islander Dance Theatre.

...

Nick Cave
Cave chose to record in Hansa studios in Berlin because it was where Bowie recorded.

Bananarama recorded a cover of the song with Stock Aitken Waterman but it was never released.

After Bowie's death, 'Changes' entered the UK singles chart for the first time, reaching number 15.

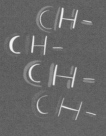

One of the most famous stutters in rock, the 'ch-ch-ch-ch' seems most likely to be an echo of 'My g-g-g-Generation' from the Who, released some six years earlier. It came out before 'b-b-b-Bennie and the Jets'.

The piano parts are performed by Rick Wakeman and played on the 100-year-old Bernstein Grand at Trident Studios, also used by Elton John and the Beatles.

Bowie played saxophone on the song and Mick Ronson arranged the strings.

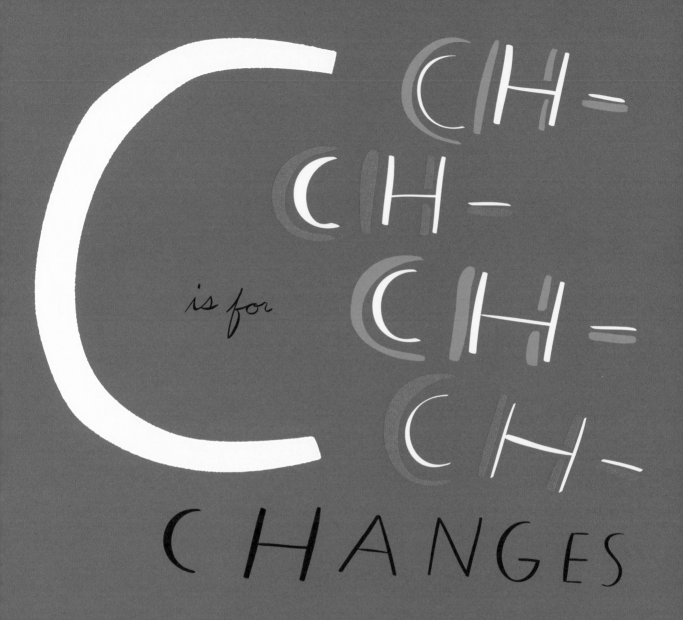

C is for

CCH–CCH–CCH–CCH–

CHANGES

From 1971's *Hunky Dory*, the song 'Changes' started out as something of a parody. However, it became a classic and was one of Bowie's most asked-for live tracks. The lyrics explore an adolescent awakening – the defiant stance of a new generation against elders who still insisted that they new best. It was written at the time when Angie Bowie was pregnant with their son Duncan, and Bowie himself was coming to grips with what would be a lifelong career of reinvention. Bowie's changes are legendary. More than any other artist, Bowie's musical persona was constantly shifting – fashion, musical style, personality and backstory all played a part, from Ziggy and Aladdin Sane, to the Thin White Duke and beyond. 'Changes' also became the name for a run of 'best-of' compilations that charted Bowie's shifting styles. *Changesonebowie* was released in 1976, *Changestwobowie* in 1981, *Changesbowie* in 1991 and finally *Nothing Has Changed* in 2014.

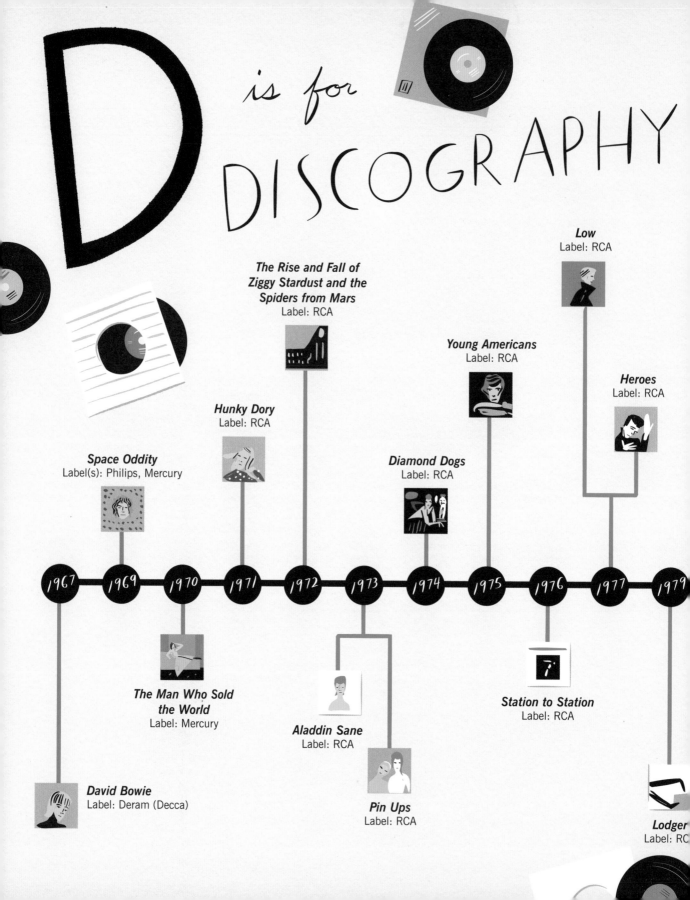

D *is for* DISCOGRAPHY

Low
Label: RCA

The Rise and Fall of Ziggy Stardust and the Spiders from Mars
Label: RCA

Young Americans
Label: RCA

Heroes
Label: RCA

Hunky Dory
Label: RCA

Diamond Dogs
Label: RCA

Space Oddity
Label(s): Philips, Mercury

1967 1969 1970 1971 1972 1973 1974 1975 1976 1977 1979

The Man Who Sold the World
Label: Mercury

Aladdin Sane
Label: RCA

Station to Station
Label: RCA

David Bowie
Label: Deram (Decca)

Pin Ups
Label: RCA

Lodger
Label: RC

You only have to look at the records released by Bowie over almost 50 years to get a sense of the man and the scope of his ambition and creativity. With no less than 25 studio albums as a solo artist, nine live albums, 49 compilation albums, 121 singles and three soundtracks, Bowie's output is staggering – but it's not just the number of albums that impresses. The stylistic shifts, inventiveness, striking visuals, identities and influences are all threaded throughout his discography. From iconic album sleeves like *Ziggy Stardust*, *Aladdin Sane* and *Heroes,* to enchanting narratives and influential shifts in style, Bowie's body of work is the story of a man constantly re-inventing himself, consistently willing to provoke, always looking for the next and the new, and somehow remaining just that little bit left of centre, even when he was a regular fixture in the charts and on commercial radio. As the man himself said, 'I don't know where I'm going from here, but I promise it won't be boring.'

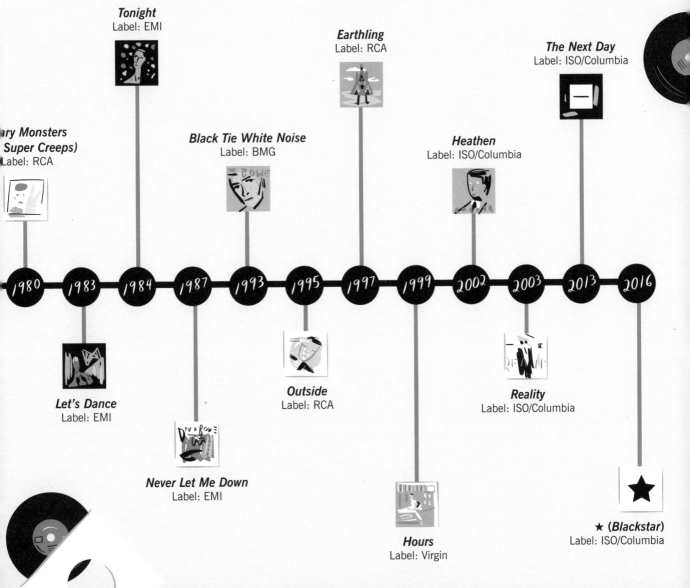

Tonight
Label: EMI

Earthling
Label: RCA

The Next Day
Label: ISO/Columbia

...ary Monsters
...Super Creeps)
Label: RCA

Black Tie White Noise
Label: BMG

Heathen
Label: ISO/Columbia

1980 *1983* *1984* *1987* *1993* *1995* *1997* *1999* *2002* *2003* *2013* *2016*

Let's Dance
Label: EMI

Outside
Label: RCA

Reality
Label: ISO/Columbia

Never Let Me Down
Label: EMI

Hours
Label: Virgin

★ **(Blackstar)**
Label: ISO/Columbia

Elephant Man
Bowie played the deformed Joseph Merrick in the Broadway production of *The Elephant Man*. Bowie famously shunned the use of any make-up or effects, choosing to portray the distorted form by using his body in artistic ways.

...

Earthling
Bowie's 20th studio album, released in 1997. Tapping into the drum-and-bass scene of the 90s, *Earthling* features frenetic drums and electronic stabs. Bowie's first self-produced LP since *Diamond Dogs,* it featured the hits 'Little Wonder', 'Dead Man Walking' and 'I'm Afraid of Americans'.

...

Extras
One of Bowie's last television performances was in Ricky Gervais' comedy series. The hilarious scene features Bowie turning Andy Millman's complaints into the song 'Little Fat Man', with a distinctively Bowie vocal flourish on the phrase 'chubby little loser'.

...

'Eight Line Poem'
This track from *Oh, You Pretty Things* features great Mick Ronson guitar work, Rick Wakeman on piano and, as the title suggests, an eight line poem from Bowie. William S. Burroughs said to Bowie, 'Well, I read this "Eight Line Poem" of yours and it is very reminiscent of T.S. Eliot.' To which Bowie replied, 'Never read him.'

...

Everybody Loves Sunshine
A relatively unknown British Independent film featuring Bowie alongside drum-and-bass pioneer Goldie. Bowie plays an aging gangster who struggles to keep peace between warring gangs on Manchester's Pepperhill Estate.

Brian Eno wrote Warszawa on his EMS 'suitcase' AKS synthesiser. The synthesiser was given to Bowie as a birthday gift after a friend obtained it later in an auction.

Happy Birthday!

Eno created the six-second start-up sound for Windows 95.

As part of their research when writing *Outside*, Bowie and Eno travelled together to Vienna to interview patients at Gugging, a psychiatric clinic that specialises in art therapy.

STOP BELIEVIN THERE IS A PROPER WAY TO DO THINGS

When writing, Eno and Bowie often utilised Peter Schmitt and Eno's 'oblique strategy cards', a set of cards containing random sayings, intended to spark creative ideas.

Eno received an email from Bowie seven days prior to his death which read: *Thank you for our good times, Brian. They will never rot.* Eno said, 'I realise now he was saying goodbye.' The email was signed 'Dawn'. Eno said they often signed off with invented names and among Bowie's others were: Mr. Showbiz, Milton Keynes, Rhoda Borrocks and The Duke of Ear.

Bowie and Brian Eno both have spiders named after them – *Heteropoda davidbowie* and *Pseudocorinna brianeno* respectively.

E is for ENO

Bowie and Brian Eno were friends and collaborators for more than 40 years, most famously working together on the albums that make up Bowie's Berlin Trilogy of *Low*, *Heroes* and *Lodger*. Eno was a pioneer of ambient music, and his new sound – febrile and spacious ambient instrumentals – were just what the musical doctor ordered at a time when Bowie was in serious need of recuperation. The one-time Roxy Music keyboardist had caught Bowie's attention with his glam-rock platform boots, feather boas and glitter. *Low* is probably seen as their highpoint, especially the sweeping instrumental 'Warszawa' which was written by Eno and played with the help of engineer Toni Visconti's four-year-old son. The two reunited on 1995's concept album *Outside*. Subtitled *The Ritual Art-Murder of Baby Grace Blue: A non-linear Gothic Drama Hyper-Cycle*, the album deals with a dystopian vision of 1999 where murder has become an art craze.

F is for FASHION

'Fashion' is, of course, a classic track from *Scary Monsters (and Super Creeps)* where Bowie mocks the shallow world of transitory fashion. It reached number five in the UK and number 70 in America. Bowie himself is synonymous with fashion, with his gender-defying avante-garde styles influencing decades of style. For the latter part of his life, Bowie's favourite designer was Rei Kawakubo of Comme des Garçons – her extraordinary sculptural and inventive haute couture fit perfectly with his aesthetic. Bowie's most notable costume designers include Michael Fish, who was responsible for the 'man dress' Bowie wore on the cover of *The Man Who Sold the World*; Freddie Buretti, who designed most of the costumes during Bowie's Ziggy era, including the ice-blue 'Life on Mars' suit; Kansai Yamamoto, the mastermind behind the iconic 'Tokyo Pop' vinyl bodysuit and the asymmetric knitted onesie from the *Aladdin Sane* tour; as well as Natasha Korniloff who interpreted Pierrot for the 'Ashes to Ashes' video and Alexander McQueen who famously designed the striking Union Jack frock coat for Bowie's *Earthling* album cover.

BEEP BEEP

Bowie first used the famous 'beep-beep' in an unreleased song called 'Rupert the Riley' in 1970.

Jean Paul Gaultier's Spring 2013 collection was an homage to Ziggy Stardust, complete with Bowie-inspired looks and catwalk models wearing red Ziggy wigs.

At age 17, Bowie appeared on a BBC program as the founder of The Society for the Prevention of Cruelty to Long-haired Men. His complaint? 'It's not nice when people call you darling and that.'

At the '75 Grammys, a coke-fuelled and near anorexic Bowie cut a sharp figure in a tuxedo, white bowtie and orange hair.

The video for 'Fashion' features May Pang, who was John Lennon's lover from '73–75 and later married Tony Visconti.

Mick Jagger once said, 'Never wear a new pair of shoes in front of him, he'll run out and buy them and they'll look better on him to boot.'

F is also for

'Fame'
Written and recorded by Bowie and John Lennon for *Young Americans*. Bowie said of he and Lennon's conversations, 'We spent endless hours talking about fame, and what it's like not having a life of your own any more. How much you want to be known before you are, and then when you are, how much you want the reverse.' He also said of fame, 'I think fame itself is not a rewarding thing. The most you can say is that it gets you a seat in restaurants.'

...

Fortune
Bowie's net worth is estimated at $230 million.

...

'Five Years'
The opening tune from *The Rise and Fall of Ziggy Stardust and the Spiders from Mars*. Its overture of doom relates to a dream Bowie had where his father told him he shouldn't fly and that he would die in five years.

...

'Friday on my Mind'
Bowie covered the classic 1965 Easybeats tune on his 1973 *Pin Ups* album. The song's co-writer Harry Vanda said it was 'the only cover I ever liked'.

...

Perry Farrell
Lead singer of Jane's Addiction and founder of Lollapalooza, Perry Farrell said of Bowie in *Rolling Stone*, 'I placed him on a godlike level. His grace on the stage was spellbinding, effortless. Music co-written with angels. Along with John Lennon, the two most inspiring men of my lifetime.' Farrell performed 'Rebel Rebel' at the Carnegie Hall Bowie tribute concert.

G
is also for

Grammys
Amazingly, Bowie only ever won two Grammys: in 1985, Best Short Form Music Video for *Jazzin' for Blue Jean* and a Lifetime Achievement Award in 2006.

...

Girlfriends (and boyfriends)
Bowie was with Hermione Farthingale in the 60s, Marianne Faithfull, 'Jean Genie' model Cyrinda Foxe, Amanda Lear, Romy Haag and Ava Cherry in the 70s. According to Susan Sarandon they had an affair in the 80s and Bowie 'toured' with 'China Girl' video model Geeling Ng. He also dated actress Melissa Hurley and had a much-reported 'fling' with Tina Turner. He dated Bianca Jagger in 1983, and possibly Mick Jagger at one stage. Other rumours include Liz Taylor, model Candy Clark, Iggy Pop, Lou Reed and Sabel Starr.

...

'Golden Years'
The famous video for this 1975 single was from *Soul Train*. Sources have said that Bowie had to get drunk for the performance as he was one of a very few white acts to ever appear on the show. Bowie said that he wanted Elvis Presley to perform it, but the singer declined.

...

Phillip Glass
Bowie was fascinated with the works of experimental composer Phillip Glass. In 1992 Glass composed a symphony based on Bowie's album *Low* called the *'Low' Symphony*. In 1996 he did the same for *Heroes*.

...

God
The last person Bowie followed on Twitter before he died was @TheTweetofGod.

All kinds of unlikely artists found themselves falling under the banner of glam rock in the 70s including the MC5, Alice Cooper, The New York Dolls, Lou Reed, Iggy Pop and Elton John.

Bowie on glam: 'I think glam rock is a lovely way to categorise me and it's even nicer to be one of the leaders of it. There's security in being part of a trend. With a little luck and if I work hard I can probably withstand it.'

'All the Young Dudes', a song Bowie wrote for Mott the Hoople, is often cited as the ultimate glam rock anthem.

ROCK AND ROLL

Bowie once asked John Lennon what he thought of glam rock and he replied, 'It's just fooking rock and roll with lipstick.'

In 2002, Bowie told the *Daily News*, 'Glam really did plant seeds for a new identity. I think a lot of kids needed that – that sense of reinvention. Kids learned that however crazy you may think it is, there is a place for what you want to do and who you want to be.'

is for
GLAM

When Marc Bolan appeared as T. Rex on *Top of the Pops* in 1971 and performed 'Hot Love' wearing glitter and satin, a new look caught the world's attention. Glam rock was a coiffured and platform boot-wearing rock and roll for the working class, and hefty stompers from acts like Gary Glitter, Wizard, The Sweet and Slade crowded the charts. At its best though, it was the expressive art rock of Bolan and Roxy Music, and, without doubt, it was transcended by its god, Ziggy Stardust. Bowie's otherworldy flamboyant and camp space junkie altered gender perceptions and gave a new meaning to performance and dressing up. Fluid gender roles would become a staple of rock and indie music from that point on. Bowie not only sidestepped the derision associated with many glam acts, but is held up as the very best of what glam had to offer. Bolan declared glam dead in 1973, but when the Spiders from Mars hit the *Top of the Pops* stage in '72 to play 'Starman' from their new LP, rock music was changed forever.

H is for HEROES

'Heroes' was co-written with Brian Eno while he and Bowie were working together in Berlin. The song deals with themes of war – specifically the Berlin Wall and how it affected everyday people. Although it is now regarded as one of Bowie's signature tunes – and certainly one of his most famous – it didn't even make the UK's Top 100 on release. The recording of the vocal sound is legendary: producer Tony Visconti set up three microphones, one 23 centimetres (9 inches) away, one 6 metres (20 feet) away and one 15 metres (50 feet) away. The microphones were gated, and only opened up when Bowie's voice hit a certain level. Add to this Robert Fripp's pitched guitar feedback and Eno's wash of synthesisers and you have a sound that has never been replicated. Bowie sang 'Heroes' at the German Reichstag in West Berlin in June 1987 and the performance – along with Bruce Springsteen's show at Radrennbahn Weissensee – is cited as contributing to the fall of the Berlin Wall. Following Bowie's death, the German government tweeted to thank him for his impact at the time and to say, 'You are now among #Heroes.'

Dave Gahan was asked to be lead singer of Depeche Mode when Vince Clarke heard him singing 'Heroes'.

On it's release *NME* journalist Charlie Gillett wrote, 'Well he had a pretty good run for our money, for a guy who was no singer. But I think his time has been and gone, and this just sounds weary.'

In 2003, Bowie said to *Performing Songwriter* of the 1987 performance, 'We kind of heard that a few of the East Berliners might actually get the chance to hear the thing, but we didn't realise in what numbers they would … So it was like a double concert where the wall was the division. And we would hear them cheering and singing along from the other side. God, even now I get choked up. It was breaking my heart. I'd never done anything like that in my life, and I guess I never will again.'

Bowie always said the song was about two lovers, one from East Berlin and one from the West. He later admitted that it was actually his producer Tony Visconti and his lover he saw kissing by the wall, which inspired the song.

The song is only certified gold in one country: Italy.

'Heroes' is Bowie's second-most covered song after 'Rebel Rebel'. Notable covers include Blondie, Peter Gabriel, TV on the Radio and Nico. The song finally got to number one in the UK and Ireland when *The X Factor* contestants of 2010 (including One Direction) released it as a charity single.

H
is also for

Hair
Teddy Antolin was Bowie's hairdresser for the past 25 years. Antolin introduced Bowie and Iman and is credited with getting him to quit smoking. He died a month after Bowie, aged 68. The famous red Ziggy/Aladdin Sane hair was done by Bowie's mum's hairdresser Suzi Fussey, who toured with Bowie and ended up marrying Mick Ronson.
…

Hunky Dory
Bowie's 4th studio LP, recorded in 1971. It was the first album to feature the line-up who would become the Spiders from Mars. Among it's many great songs were 'Changes' and 'Oh! You Pretty Things', plus the eponymously-titled tribute to Andy Warhol.
…

Hermione
Bowie's former lover Hermione Farthingale broke his heart and became the subject of 'Letter to Hermione' from *Space Oddity* and is the 'girl with the mousy hair' referenced in 'Life on Mars'.
…

Hitler
Bowie held a fascination for Nazi history and was once quoted as saying, 'When you think about it, Adolf Hitler was the first pop star.' He was also famously snapped at Victoria Station doing what many believed looked suspiciously like a Nazi salute while getting out of his car. Bowie flatly denied the Nazi salute (saying he was just caught 'mid-wave') and has since stated that his bizarre claims about Hitler were made when he was going through a very dark time.

is also for

Iggy Pop

Stooges lead singer Iggy Pop joined Bowie in Berlin in the 70s. During this time Bowie co-wrote and produced his albums *The Idiot* and *Lust for Life*. The two were lifelong friends, and Iggy once said of Bowie, 'This guy salvaged me from certain professional and maybe personal annihilation – simple as that.'

...

Isolar and *Isolar II*

Bowie's 1976 and 1978 world tours. The first was in support of *Station to Station* the second *Low* and *Heroes*.

...

'I Got You Babe'

Bowie performed a version of the Sonny and Cher song on *The Midnight Special* with Marianne Faithfull in 1973. It was the last time he ever publicly appeared as Ziggy.

...

'I Can't Explain'

A 1965 single from The Who, which Bowie recorded for his 1973 covers album, *Pin Ups*.

...

Icon

When BBC's *The Culture Show* held a public vote in 2006, Bowie was voted fourth in Britain's Greatest Living Icons behind Paul McCartney, Morrissey and David Attenborough at number one.

...

Introvert

Bowie was quite shy and introverted offstage, in interviews and behind the scenes. He told *Fresh Air*'s Terry Gross in 2002, 'Frankly, if I could get away with not having to perform, I'd be very happy. It's not my favourite thing to do. What I like doing is writing and recording ... I don't live for the stage. I don't live for an audience.'

Bowie said of Iman and himself on the birth of their daughter, 'Overnight, our lives have been enriched beyond belief."

Bowie and Iman both appeared in the video game *Omikron: the Nomad Soul*, for which Bowie created the soundtrack.

Iman once wore a Ziggy Stardust T-shirt when hosting *Project Runway*.

Bowie proposed to Iman in Paris under the Pont Neuf.

Iman once said in an interview with *Harper's Bazaar*, 'I'm not married to David Bowie, I'm married to David Jones. I've never had members of the press in my apartment. At home, it's home. You retain the difference between a person and a persona.'

I is for IMAN

Despite both appearing in the film *The Linguini Incident*, Bowie and Iman didn't really meet until Bowie's long-time stylist Teddy Antolin introduced them at a party. Antolin said, 'The minute [Iman] walked in, all the attention went to her. She had a big smile and her and David looked at each other and it was love at first sight, you could feel the electricity, something went off.' They were married in 1992, and their daughter Alexandria was born in 2000. They were married for 23 years. Iman Mohamed Abdulmajid is a Somali-born model, actress and founder and CEO of IMAN Cosmetics. Iman is Arabic for 'Faith' and her religion is Muslim. She had been married twice before Bowie, once to a Somali entrepreneur and once to an American professional basketball player with whom she has a daughter, Zulekha. Bowie said of their relationship, 'You would think that a rock star being married to a supermodel would be one of the greatest things in the world. It is.'

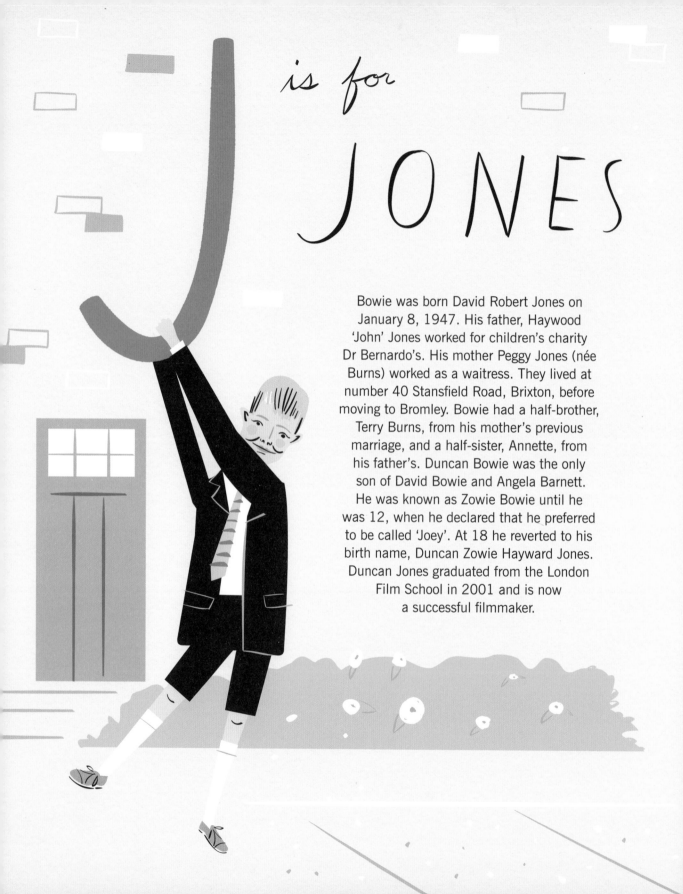

is for

JONES

Bowie was born David Robert Jones on January 8, 1947. His father, Haywood 'John' Jones worked for children's charity Dr Bernardo's. His mother Peggy Jones (née Burns) worked as a waitress. They lived at number 40 Stansfield Road, Brixton, before moving to Bromley. Bowie had a half-brother, Terry Burns, from his mother's previous marriage, and a half-sister, Annette, from his father's. Duncan Bowie was the only son of David Bowie and Angela Barnett. He was known as Zowie Bowie until he was 12, when he declared that he preferred to be called 'Joey'. At 18 he reverted to his birth name, Duncan Zowie Hayward Jones. Duncan Jones graduated from the London Film School in 2001 and is now a successful filmmaker.

Duncan Jones' instant-classic sci-fi flick *Moon* won a slew of awards, including a BAFTA for outstanding debut and a British Independent Film Award.

David's half brother Terry was ten years older than Bowie; Terry introduced him to jazz music and was very influential during Bowie's childhood.

Bowie's parents married eight months after his birth. They were waiting for his father's divorce to come through.

Terry suffered from schizophrenia and eventually committed suicide by lying in front of a train. Bowie didn't attend his funeral for fear of creating a media circus, but sent flowers with a note saying, 'You've seen more things than we can imagine, but all these moments will be lost – like tears washed away by the rain,' paraphrasing a famous line from the film *Blade Runner*.

Bowie changed his name when he was 18, in order to avoid confusion with singer Davy Jones, who went on to become the front man for The Monkees.

Mick Jagger
Bowie was clearly enamoured with the lead singer of The Rolling Stones and their on-again, off-again friendship is the stuff of rock legend. No one knows for sure if they actually had a physical relationship and both have denied it repeatedly. In her book *Backstage Passes: Life on the Wild Side with David Bowie*, Angie Bowie more than hints that Jagger and Bowie were lovers, and Bowie's former girlfriend Ava Cherry claims to have been 'the filling in a David Bowie and Mick Jagger cookie'.

...

Japan
Bowie was heavily influenced by Japanese designers and Kabuki theatre. The band Japan were heavily influenced by Bowie, and lead singer David Sylvian contributed vocals to 'Forbidden Colours' from the Bowie film *Merry Christmas Mr. Lawrence*.

...

'John, I'm Only Dancing'
Released initially in September 1972 and backed with Ziggy album track 'Hang on to Yourself' this excellent single openly addressed gay and bisexual relationships and was deemed too risqué to be released as a single in the USA.

...

'The Jean Genie'
The lead single from *Aladdin Sane* reached number two in the UK charts in 1972. In the book *Moonage Daydream* Bowie said, 'Starting out as a lightweight riff thing I had written one evening in NY for Cyrinda's [Cyrinda Foxe, the Warhol associate who starred in the video] enjoyment, I developed the lyric to the otherwise wordless pumper and it ultimately turned into a bit of a smorgasbord of imagined Americana ... based on an Iggy-type persona ... The title, of course, was a clumsy pun upon Jean Genet.'

K
is also for

Nick Kent
Infamous British rock critic Nick Kent said of Bowie, 'Bowie didn't invent glam rock – Marc Bolan and Alice Cooper had both predated him as hit-making ambassadors of the form – but he was its prettiest and most musically accomplished human asset and, moreover, possessed the requisite charisma and lightning intelligence to change the whole course of popular music that year.' Bowie had once said to Kent, 'So you're Nick Kent, aren't you pretty?' and blew him a kiss.

...

Knighthood
Bowie declined a Knighthood in 2003 (he had previously declined a CBE in 2000), saying, 'I would never have any intention of accepting anything like that. It's not what I spent my life working for.'

...

Kooks
Appearing on 1971's *Hunky Dory* 'Kooks' was written for Bowie's newborn son Zowie/Duncan.

...

Kashmir
Bowie sung on the Danish band's single 'The Cynic' which was produced by Tony Visconti. Visconti introduced them at a Killers concert. Visconti said, 'When I introduced David to Kasper in the balcony VIP section and told him he was the lead singer of Kashmir, David enthusiastically shook his hand saying that he had already heard their last CD and liked it.'

Kemp cast Bowie as a dancer in the BBC production *The Pistol Shot*, which is where he met Hermione Farthingale, the subject of the song 'Letter to Hermione'.

One of Kemp's early stage performances was in *Pierrot in Turquoise* – the Pierrot motif would later pop up in Bowie's work, most notably in his 'Ashes to Ashes' video.

Lindsay Kemp appeared onstage with Bowie in the *Ziggy Stardust* shows at the Rainbow Theatre.

Kemp appears in the Mick Rock directed video for 'John I'm Only Dancing', which was banned by *Top of the Pops*.

Bowie was not the only famous student of Kemp: Kate Bush also got some of her moves from him.

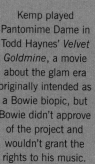

Kemp played Pantomime Dame in Todd Haynes' *Velvet Goldmine*, a movie about the glam era originally intended as a Bowie biopic, but Bowie didn't approve of the project and wouldn't grant the rights to his music.

K is for KEMP

Bowie studied under Lindsay Kemp in 1967, enrolling in his class at the Dance Centre in London to study mime and underground theatre. This experience not only provided Bowie with some of his signature moves, but also helped him develop some of his most enduring characters. Bowie said of Kemp, 'His day-to-day life was the most theatrical thing I had ever seen, ever. It was everything I thought bohemia probably was. I joined the circus.' Lindsay Kemp was born in Cheshire in 1938 and loved dance from an early age. He went on to study mime under Marcel Marceau and formed his own dance company in the early 60s. Rupert Smith of *The Guardian* described Kemp's style as a mixture of 'hard-knocks realism' with erotic flights of fantasy. No wonder it appealed to Bowie.

L is for LABYRINTH

This fantasy adventure film was made in 1986 and directed by Muppets creator Jim Henson. Bowie played the punk glam Jareth, aka The Goblin King. With frightwig hair like a spidery waterfall and an all-too revealing codpiece, The Goblin King has become one of Bowie's most enduring images despite the film being a box office failure. The acting wouldn't win any awards and the best known song from the Bowie-penned soundtrack is the oh-so 80s 'Magic Dance', but the playfulness and absurdist humour of the film (the screenplay was written by Monty Python's Terry Jones), along with Henson and Bowie's cult status, have turned it into a pop-culture lynchpin for 80s and 90s revivalists. For children of the 80s, *Labyrinth* was likely their first foray into Bowiedom.

Jareth the Goblin King was originally intended to be a puppet as well.

Sting, Michael Jackson, Mick Jagger and Prince were all considered for the role of the Jareth.

Bowie described himself at 17 as a 'mime trapped inside a man's body'. He used his mime skills to great effect in *Labyrinth*.

The track 'Underground' was released as a single and a music video that utilised many of the puppets and themes from *Labyrinth*, but did not contain any footage from the actual film.

Lumpy dwarf puppet Hoggle was lost in transit. *Labyrinth* fans can find him in a glass case at the Unclaimed Baggage Centre in Alabama.

All of the baby noises in the song 'Magic Dance' were made by Bowie himself.

L is also for

Low
From Bowie's self-fulfilling prophesy of post punk and new wave, to Brian Eno's Synthi washes and Visconti's innovative production, this LP influenced a generation and still sounds cutting-edge to this day.

...

'Liza Jane'
Bowie's first single ever! Released under the name David Jones and the King Bees. Released in 1964 when Bowie was 17, it was not a chart success. An original copy sold in 2011 for US$3,000.

...

'The Laughing Gnome'
This novelty song from 1967 went to number six in the charts. When Bowie asked fans to request songs for his 1990 tour via text, it was the most requested song. He didn't play it. He was a star by the time it was re-released and became a hit and he always described it as 'an embarrassment'.

...

Lust for Life
In 1977 Bowie co-wrote and played on Iggy Pop's classic LP.

...

Let's Dance
The title track of Bowie's 1983 LP reached number one in the UK and the USA and was accompanied by a ground-breaking music video. Co-produced by Chic's Nile Rodgers, the album also featured Bowie's version of the Iggy Pop/Bowie-penned 'China Girl'. Despite its commercial appeal, there are some oddball numbers on the album, such as the frenetic 'Ricochet' and the moody 'Criminal World'.

M *is also for*

'Modern Love'
The third single from *Let's Dance*, released in 1983. It reached number two on the UK charts.

....

The Man Who Sold the World
Bowie's third LP is the pivot point between the pastoral leanings of *Space Oddity* and the glam rock of *Ziggy Stardust*. It also marks the point where Bowie's obsession with Crowley, Nietzsche and Kafka started creeping into his themes. Notable covers of the title track were by Lulu, who had a hit with it in 1974, and by Nirvana on their unplugged LP.

...

'Moonage Daydream'
A power chord-laden track from *The Rise and fall of Ziggy Stardust and the Spiders from Mars* featuring one of guitarist Mick Ronson's most memorable solos. It was first released as a single by Bowie's side-project Arnold Corns in 1971.

...

Make-up
Bowie's mother Peggy recalled finding a very small David Bowie 'covered' in make-up. She said, 'When I found him, he looked for all the world like a clown. I told him, "You shouldn't use make-up" but he said, "You do, Mummy." I agreed but pointed out that it wasn't for little boys.'

...

Mug shot
Bowie and Iggy pop were busted for marijuana possession in 1976. They were released without charge, the result for Bowie was one of the most stylish mug shots of all time.

...

Midwife
The midwife who delivered baby Bowie fancied herself a clairvoyant. When he was born she reportedly said, 'This child has been on Earth before'.

...

George Martin
The famous Beatles producer declined when offered the job of producing Bowie's *Space Oddity* LP.

Bowie was offered the role of Captain Hook in Steven Spielberg's *Hook*, but he turned it down (the role went to Dustin Hoffman).

Ben Stiller described working with Bowie during his cameo in *Zoolander* as a high point in his career.

Films inspired by Bowie include Todd Haynes' *Velvet Goldmine*, and *A Bigger Splash*, which features Bowie's friend and doppelganger Tilda Swinton.

FILMOGRAPHY

The Image 1967 (short film)
Theatre 625 1968
The Virgin Soldiers 1969
The Looking Glass Murders 1970
Ziggy Stardust and the Spiders From Mars 1973
The Man Who Fell to Earth 1975 (Saturn Award, Best Actor)

Just a Gigolo 1978
Christiane F 1971
The Snowman 1982
Baal 1982
Merry Christmas Mr. Lawrence 1983
The Hunger 1983
Yellowbeard 1983
Into the Night 1985
Labyrinth 1986

Absolute Beginners 1986
The Last Temptation of Christ 1988
Dream on 1991
The Linguini Incident 1991
Twin Peaks: Fire Walk With Me 1992
Basquiat 1996
Gunslinger's Revenge 1998

Everybody Love's Sunshine 1999
Mr. Rice's Secret 2000
Zoolander 2001
The Prestige 2006
Arthur and the Invisibles 2007
Spongebob's Atlantis Squarepantis 2007
August 2008
Bandslam 2009

Bowie loved his costumes from *The Man Who Fell to Earth* so much, he kept them to wear on his *Station to Station* tour.

In *Just a Gigolo* Bowie starred alongside Marlene Dietrich in the last film of her career. However, they were never in the same place at the same time – their scenes were shot separately and then cut together.

M

is for

MOVIE STAR

Bowie's theatrical stage persona and love of theatre led him to many unique acting roles – many of which were as iconic as they were idiosyncratic. He has more films to his credit than albums, and, while his film performances were never as critically acclaimed as his musical ones, his screen presence was always electrifying and many of his movies retain cult followings. Bowie's film career spanned an extraordinary variety of characters, ranging from real-world heroes such as Nikola Tesla and Andy Warhol, to the fantastical realms of aliens, vampires and goblin kings. He won a Saturn award for best actor for *The Man Who Fell to Earth*, while his performance in *Merry Christmas Mr. Lawrence* is widely regarded as his best.

is for

NEWLEY

Often cited by Bowie himself as a major influence on his earlier work, Anthony Newley was a singer–songwriter and actor in the 60s. Newley was born in 1931 and had 12 hits between 1959 and 1962, including 'Feeling Good' which was later covered by Nina Simone. Newley co-wrote the theme to *Goldfinger* and the score to 1971's *Willy Wonka and the Chocolate Factory*. He had also portrayed the artful dodger in the 1948 film version of *Oliver Twist*. He sang with a very British accent and his sound always contained a thread of melancholy, which helped shape the musical style of the young Bowie. Newley's sound can be heard all over Bowie's self-titled debut album and *Space Oddity*, and Newley's theatrical, music-hall persona was a huge influence on Bowie. Newley was inducted into the Songwriters Hall of Fame in 1989.

Bowie was a big fan of Newley's TV show, *The Strange World of Gurney Slade*.

Bowie recorded a cover of 'What Kind of Fool Am I?' for the 2003 Anthony Newley tribute album *Pop Goes the Weasel*.

In 1968, Mike Vernon, the in-house producer for Decca was given the job of making Bowie's first record. 'I had never heard of him,' Vernon said. 'My first reaction was: he's a young Anthony Newley. There was a dramatic, show-tune influence in the songs and a storytelling approach that was unique at the time.'

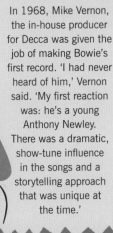

Bowie's 'Laughing Gnome' was a clear pastiche of Newley's vaudevile songs. He was known for swinging versions of old tunes like 'Pop Goes the Weasel'.

N

is also for

The Next Day
Bowie's 24th studio album, released March 2013. It was his first album in ten years, and gained Bowie his first number one in the UK since the 1993 release of *Black Tie, White Noise*. The cover art is the cover of *Heroes*, obscured by a white square containing the album's title. Producer and bass player Tony Visconti said that during recording breaks he would listen to the demos, 'I was walking around New York with my headphones on, looking at all the people with Bowie T-shirts on thinking, boy, if you only knew what I'm listening to at the moment.'

...

Nathan Adler
A character invented by Bowie whose 'diary' features in the liner notes for 1995's *Outside*. Adler is a gumshoe noir detective in a dystopian future where murder has become 'art'.

...'

Nine Inch Nails
Bowie chose the industrial outfit as his co-headline on the *Outside* tour. Bowie contributed vocals to their song 'Hurt'.

...

Nirvana
Nirvana covered 'The Man Who Sold the World' for their album, *MTV Unplugged in New York*. Bowie said of Nirvana's cover, 'I was simply blown away when I found that Kurt Cobain liked my work, and have always wanted to talk to him about his reasons for covering "The Man Who Sold the World". It would have been nice to have worked with him, but just talking with him would have been real cool.'

O

is also for

Outside

This album marked the first time Bowie had worked with Brian Eno since the 'Berlin Trilogy.' The liner notes feature a short story, *The Diary of Nathan Adler*. The album spawned three hit singles, most notable 'Hallo Spaceboy', which was very well received when remixed by The Pet Shop Boys. After Bowie's death, Eno said, 'About a year ago we started talking about *Outside* – the last album we worked on together. We talked about revisiting it, taking it somewhere new. I was looking forward to that.'

...

Omikron: The Nomad Soul

A video game developed by Quantic Dream. Bowie provided the music and several songs, some which were to appear later as B-sides to singles from the album *Hours*. He had input into the storyline and game design, and appeared twice in the game, once as a character called Bos, and once as the lead singer of a fictional band called The Dreamers. Iman also had a small part in the game.

...

'O' Levels

Bowie got 'O' Levels in art and woodwork.

...

Occult

In LA in the 70s Bowie became heavily addicted to cocaine, which led to a very real paranoia and obsession with the occult. He was reportedly reading a book called *Psychic Self-Defence,* a manual for guarding yourself against 'paranormal malevolence'. He began drawing protective pentagrams on every surface. Many think that the line in 'Breaking Glass': *Don't look at the carpet. I drew something awful on it*, refers to one of those pentagrams. Bowie himself said, 'My psyche went through the roof. I was hallucinating 24 hours a day.'

The song was also recorded by Peter Noone of Herman's Hermits. His version reached number 12 in the UK charts in 1971. Bowie played piano on his version. Noone changed the line *the Earth is a bitch*, to *the Earth is a beast*.

Bowie possibly signalled the end of the reign of the pretty things on his 1999 album *Hours*, with the track 'The Pretty Things are Going to Hell'. In the video he meets past versions of himself: The Man Who Sold the World, Ziggy, The Thin White Duke and Pierrot.

Bowie often performed the song live as a medley with 'Wild Eyed Boy from Freecloud' and 'All the Young Dudes'.

The song's piano intro has often been compared to The Beatles track 'Martha My Dear'.

On first reporting on his bisexuality, the local British papers ran the headline, 'Oh, You Pretty Thing' forever linking the song to Bowie's sexuality.

Pierre LaRoche is the make-up artist credited with adorning Bowie with his definitive Aladdin Sane lightning bolt, as well as Ziggy's golden 'astral sphere'. LaRoche said of Bowie in '73, 'He has the perfect face for make-up. He has even features, high cheekbones and a very good mouth.' Post-Bowie, LaRoche went on to create the iconic looks for the *Rocky Horror Picture Show.*

is for

OH! YOU PRETTY THINGS

Bowie released this track as a single from *Hunky Dory* in December 1971. The song's themes of youth aligning themselves with a visiting alien race, also reflected upon on in 'Starman', seem to be Bowie's take on Nietzsche and occultist Aleister Crowley's visions of the decline of the human race – it also suggests that Bowie was heralding in a new age where the old guard's rigid ways were replaced by a youth with a more fluid take on politics, fashion and sexuality.

P is for PIN UPS

Bowie's seventh LP was an album of covers and the last to feature the Spiders from Mars as his backing band (although drummer Mick Woodmansey was replaced by Aynsley Dunbar). *Pin Ups* is Bowie's tribute to many of the acts he considered to be an influence on his music. There were two songs apiece by The Who and The Yardbirds, and a cover of Pink Floyd's 'See Emily Play' seemed natural as Syd Barret was another left-of-centre character who sang in a pronounced English accent. There were also covers of Them, The Kinks, The Easybeats, The Pretty Things and The Mojos. Bowie's stunning cover of 'Sorrow' by the Merseys was so good that it's thought of today as one of his classic songs. Notable heroes of Bowie left off the album include Elvis, Bob Dylan Marc Bolan, Mick Jagger and John Lennon, although Bowie later famously covered The Beatles' 'Across the Universe' and The Rolling Stones' 'Let's Spend The Night Together'. Bowie himself has been covered countless times, by acts as diverse as Nirvana, Barbara Streisand, Tori Amos, The White Stripes, The Cure, Matchbox 20, Janelle Monae, Peter Gabriel, Duran Duran, Robbie Williams, Phillip Glass and Beck, to name just a few.

The album cover features Bowie and model Twiggy, photographed by Twiggy's then manager, Justin de Villeneuve. Originally intended for *Vogue*, Bowie liked the shot so much he took it for the album cover. De Villeneuve has said, 'When I got back to London and told *Vogue*, they never spoke to me again.'

Pin Ups entered the charts the same day as Bryan Ferry's covers album *These Foolish Things*. The omission of some of Bowie's heroes such as Elvis, John Lennon and The Rolling Stones is thought to be because Ferry covered most of these artists on his record.

WHITELIGHT/
WHITE HEAT
THE VELVET UNDERGROUND

A version of The Velvet Underground's 'White Light, White Heat' was recorded but left off the album.

A version of Bruce Springsteen's 'Growin' Up' and Jacques Brel's 'Port of Amsterdam' were included on the 1990 re-release.

P
is also for

Punk
Although Bowie generally absorbed each new musical style as it came along, he seemed to miss punk rock completely. In an interview with the Australian press in 1978, Bowie said, 'To define it as punk, you're automatically putting a boundary around what's possible.' He also name-checked Talking Heads as a great punk band but added, 'Oh, there's a new band I saw the other day … Dire Straits?'

…

Paintings
Bowie told the *New York Times* in 1998 that, 'Art was, seriously, the only thing I'd ever wanted to own. It can change the way that I feel in the mornings.' He owned two Tintorettos and a Rubens, and was also a collector of the work of Tracy Emin and Damien Hirst. He was a big fan of painters Francis Picabia, Egon Schiele and Francis Bacon. Bowie himself was an accomplished painter with an expressionistic style very influenced by Bacon and Picabia.

…

Plastic Soul
Bowie described his early-to-mid 70s recordings as 'plastic soul', a term used to describe white artists singing soul music. Bowie had a life-long love of soul and R&B, saying they were 'the bedrock of all popular music'.

…

Elvis Presley
Elvis changed Bowie's life forever. Bowie said that he saw a cousin dancing to 'Hound Dog' and was amazed by the power of music. The musicians shared the same birthday, and the unreleased Presley tune 'Blackstar' and its premonition of death, was said to be a major influence on Bowie's final album.

Q is also for

'Queen Bitch'

This song, written in 1971 for *Hunky Dory*, was described by Bowie as a tribute to Lou Reed. It's very similar in style to the Velvet Underground; in particular their song 'Sweet Jane', although Bowie said the riff was inspired by Eddie Cochrane's 'Three Steps to Heaven'. Either way, it was the blueprint for the glam-rock sound of *The Rise and Fall of Ziggy Stardust and the Spiders From Mars*.

...

Quiff

Bowie started his musical career with a quiff and a skinny suit and tie, very much a traditional mod. He revived the hairstyle in the 80s, but adding tails and a bouffant.

...

Queen Elizabeth

Bowie turned down a knighthood from the Queen of England. His said, 'I seriously don't know what it's for.'

...

Quirks

While it's widely known that Bowie chain-smoked, had an obsessive interest in the occult and Kabbalah and liked to draw protective runes and pentagrams, some of Bowie's lesser-known quirks include his fondness for shepherd's pie, the fact that he never drank tea (unless it was Japanese green tea), and during the recording of *Station to Station* he lived on a diet of cocaine, peppers and milk.

The track originally peaked on the US Billboard chart at number 29. After Bowie's death it re-entered the chart for one week at number 45.

It was at the Freddy Mercury tribute concert where Bowie got down on one knee and recited The Lord's Prayer. Brian May said no one knew it was going to happen and described it as a 'show-stopping moment'.

Vanilla Ice famously used the riff for his 90s hit 'Ice Ice Baby'.

Everyone contributed vocals at first and the song had a working title of 'People on Streets', but Bowie decided to take over the lyrics and song structure at that point. Queen were happy to relinquish control as May says, 'Bowie was having a genius moment.'

Queen bass player John Deacon credits Bowie with coming up with the bass-line riff. Later accounts lean towards Deacon coming up with the riff but then forgetting it while out to dinner. Luckily Bowie remembered it. Brian May recalled a tense moment where Bowie stopped Deacon from playing to show him the right way to play the riff. The lyrics were mostly written by Bowie.

Queen played the track live at every one of their concerts from 1981 until they stopped touring in 1986, but Bowie didn't perform it live until the Freddy Mercury tribute concert, where Annie Lennox sang Mercury's lines. After that he performed it regularly, with bass player Gail Ann Dorsey taking Mercury's role.

Queen's guitarist Brian May said of the writing and recording of the song, 'It was hard, because you had four very precocious boys and David, who was precocious enough for all of us.'

is for
QUEEN

Bowie collaborated with Queen on the single 'Under Pressure' in 1981. It ended up as the final track on Queen's 1982 album *Hot Space*. With the two legendary vocalists, Freddy Mercury – operatic, flamboyant and camp – and Bowie – theatrical, enigmatic and tortured – the result couldn't fail to be something special. It was a coincidence that they got together: Queen just happened to be in Montreux in Switzerland at the time Bowie was living there. Bowie popped in to the studio to say hello and the band asked him to contribute vocals to a Queen song called 'Cool Cat'. He didn't like his voice on the track, so instead he started to jam over a piece Queen was working on called 'Feel Like'. 'Under Pressure' was the result. It was Bowie's third UK number one after 'Space Oddity' in 1969 and 'Ashes to Ashes' in 1980, and it was Queen's second UK number one – the first since 'Bohemian Rhapsody' in 1975.

is for

R REBEL REBEL

Bowie was an icon of rebellion, railing (always elegantly) against society's notions of gender and sexuality. Joe Moran said about him in *The Guardian*, 'The world was changing, but not fast enough. While a pop star putting his arm around another man on television might not look very revolutionary now, it seems to have been a liberating moment for young people coming to terms with their sexualities.' It's no wonder one of his most enduring tracks is a rallying cry for misfits. 'Rebel Rebel' was released in 1974, a single from *Diamond Dogs*. Despite being released at a time when Bowie was leaving his glam persona behind, it was a bit of a glam rock stomper and this had immediate appeal for fans. The song went to number five in the UK. It's Bowie's most-covered song, and of the many covers, among the *least* notable are by Bryan Adams, Bay City Rollers and Shaun Cassidy. Even Dead or Alive and Duran Duran had a go, but nobody did it justice. It makes a nice bookend with its re-release B-side 'Queen Bitch' – the song that heralded Bowie's glam rock era, while 'Rebel Rebel' brought it to a close.

The original version makes reference to Quaaludes. Bowie re-recorded the song in 2003 and left the reference out.

The riff has been likened to a Keith Richards 'Satisfaction'-style guitar hook. Bowie said, 'It's a fabulous riff! Just fabulous! When I stumbled onto it, it was "Oh, thank you!"'

The original version goes for four and a half minutes. A much more punchy US version was released later which ran around two and a half minutes.

It was Bowie's first hit since 1969 not to feature Mick Ronson. Bowie played the guitar on the track.

'Rebel Rebel' was written for a Ziggy Stardust musical that never got off the ground.

ZIGGY STARDUST the musical

ADMIT ONE
ADMIT ONE

R
is also for

Religion
Bowie married Iman in a private ceremony in 1992 but felt that they should have a real marriage, 'sanctified by God', which took place in a church in Florence. Earlier that year, he knelt on stage and recited the Lord's Prayer at the Freddy Mercury Tribute Concert before a TV audience of nearly one billion people. In 1993, Bowie said he had an 'undying' belief in the 'unquestionable' existence of God. However, when he was interviewed in 2005, Bowie said the question of God's existence 'is not a question that can be answered ... I'm not quite an atheist and it worries me. There's that little bit that holds on: "Well, I'm *almost* an atheist. Give me a couple of months."'

...

Rabbit
Reportedly, while on tour in North America in 2004, Bowie was stalked by someone dressed in a pink rabbit costume. He laughed it off at the time, but was said to be disturbed when he boarded the plane to leave New York and the bunny, still in costume, was on board.

...

Reality
Bowie's 23rd studio LP, released in 2003 on his own label ISO records. Co-produced by Bowie and Tony Visconti, the album featured a central premise of reality vs illusion, and posed the question of whether or not reality really existed anymore. The album features two covers – The Modern Lovers' 'Pablo Picasso' and George Harrison's 'Try Some, Buy One' – both slated for the unrealised album *Pin Ups 2*. *Reality* reached number three in the UK, but it went to number one in Denmark.

S is also for

'Starman'
A late addition to *The Rise and Fall of Ziggy Stardust and the Spiders from Mars* when RCA's Dennis Katz insisted that the album needed a single.

...

Scary Monsters
Bowie's 14th studio LP released in 1980. The back cover reveals the added title *(and Super Creeps)*. The album features two of Bowie's all-time classics 'Ashes to Ashes' and 'Fashion'.

...

Station to Station
Bowie's tenth studio LP released in 1976. The album introduced one of his most well-known characters, the Thin White Duke, and included the classics 'Golden Years' and 'Wild is the Wind'.

...

'Suffragette City'
Originally appearing on *The Rise and Fall of Ziggy Stardust and the Spiders From Mars*, the song was later released as a single to plug the *Changesonebowie* best-of compilation.

...

Synthesiser
Bowie was a synthesiser obsessive, from his use of the Mellotron (thanks to studio muso at the time, Rick Wakeman) on *Space Oddity,* to *Ashes to Ashes* and beyond. The Synthi AKS used on *Low* was the same one used by Pink Floyd for *Dark Side of the Moon*'s instrumental 'On the Run'.

...

Saxophone
Bowie played the alto sax on a lot of his recordings, although it was David Sanborn who plays the famous riff on 'Young Americans'.

Flight of the Conchords paid tribute to their love of Bowie with the cheeky 'Bowie's in Space' from episode six of the HBO comedy series.

'Space Oddity' reached number three on the iTunes chart two days after Bowie's death.

Advertisements used the track to promote the Stylophone, which Bowie plays in the first verse.

Famed keyboardist Rick Wakeman from prog rock band Yes was a session musician during the recording of 'Space Oddity' and played Mellotron on the track.

BBC radio didn't play the single until the Apollo 11 astronauts had returned safely.

Astronaut Chris Hadfield recorded a version of the song while on the International Space Station – making it the first music video to be shot in space.

Two Belgian astronomers (and fans) named a constellation after him. The Bowie Constellation is near Mars and when traced out is shaped like the iconic Ziggy lightening bolt. There was also a push to name Planet 9 (a new planet discovered in the week of Bowie's death) 'Planet Bowie'.

is for

SPACE ODDITY

First released in 1969, this tripped-out anthem was Bowie's first bona fide hit. It got to number five in the UK charts and garnered Bowie a joint Ivor Novello award for best songwriting that year (shared with, of all things, Peter Sarstedt's 'Where Do You Go To, (My Lovely?)'). It was the year of the moon landing and interest in space and technology was high, but Bowie's influence was more specifically Stanley Kubrik's monumental film *2001: A Space Odyssey*. In his own words, 'I was very stoned when I went to see it, several times, and it was really a revelation to me.' Bowie's eponymous second LP was renamed *Space Oddity* in 1972 and on re-release of the track in 1975 (on maxi single) 'Space Oddity' landed at number one on the UK charts. The song introduced Major Tom, who reappeared in Bowie's classic 'Ashes to Ashes', the Pet Shop Boys' reworking of the single 'Hallo Spaceboy' and was arguably, finally put to rest in the video for 'Blackstar'.

T is for THIN WHITE DUKE

Primarily associated with his 1976 album *Station to Station*, Bowie's slick and stylish Thin White Duke was conceived at a time when Bowie was deeply fascinated by occultist Aleister Crowley, Nazi imagery and Friedrich Nietzsche's concept of the *Übermensch*. Bowie described him as a 'very Aryan, fascist type; a would-be romantic with absolutely no emotion at all but who spouted a lot of neo-romance'. After Bowie made some bizarre comments to the press about Hitler and facism, the Thin White Duke began to take on very sinister connotations. Bowie was heavily addicted to cocaine during this time and blamed the drug use and his unstable state of mind for the more bizarre elements of his behaviour (including a habit of drawing pentagrams and protective runes wherever he went). In an attempt to escape his addiction, Bowie killed off The Thin White Duke and decamped from Los Angeles to the relative anonymity of Berlin.

Bowie later described the Thin White Duke as 'a very nasty character indeed' and 'an emotionless Aryan superman'.

Tin Machine
Formed in 1991, Tin Machine was a band put together by Bowie featuring guitarist Reeves Gabrels and brothers Tony and Hunt Sales. Unofficial fifth member Kevin Armstrong has since worked with Morrissey. Bowie set it up following the desire to be a member of a band rather than a solo performer. Tin Machine lasted only two years before Bowie decided that being a solo performer was his thing. Despite being generally considered as Bowie's lowest point, the band sold two million albums and Bowie has stated that his time with the band revitalised his career.

...

'Telling Lies'
Bowie made this single from his *Earthling* album available to download in 1996 – making him the first major artist to release a single online. Reportedly, it took about 11 minutes to download the song using dial-up internet.

...

Tattoos
Bowie had one tattoo on his left calf, an image of a dolphin with a Japanese serenity prayer inscribed around it in kanji. He drew it himself and got a Japanese tattoo artist to ink it for him. Iman has a small bowie knife tattooed above her ankle with the word David written in it as well as the Arabic lettering for David around her belly button.

...

Tina Turner
Bowie not only reportedly had a fling with the soul singer but they also co-wrote and recorded the song 'Girls' which features on Turner's LP *Break Every Rule*.

Bowie tried to distance himself from the Thin White Duke's persona by saying, 'What you see on stage isn't sinister. It's pure clown. I'm using myself as a canvas and trying to paint the truth of our time on it. The white face, the baggy pants – they're Pierrot, the eternal clown putting over the great sadness.'

Getting out of his car outside Victoria Station, and dressed in a brown shirt and with a head of swept-back blonde hair, Bowie was photographed making what some alleged to be a Nazi salute to his fans. Bowie said he was simply waving and the photographer captured him mid-wave.

The Thin White Duke was based in part on Jerome Thomas Newton, Bowie's character in *The Man Who Fell to Earth*

THE MAN WHO FELL TO EARTH
526 2

Later Bowie described the character and the recording of *Station to Station* as his 'darkest days'. He said of his habit, 'I was out of my mind, totally crazed.'

U

is also for

Underpants

After Bowie died, Brian Eno posted a picture of Bowie in his underpants playing the saxophone on Twitter with the hashtag #GreatestEverDavidBowiePic.

...

'Underground'

The gospel-infused 'Underground' was released as a single from the *Labyrinth* soundtrack. The video clip (which Bowie didn't much care for) is live action that segues into animation, a style that director Steve Barron used in his famous video for A-ha's 'Take On Me'.

...

Underworld

Bowie appears on the soundtrack to the 2003 film starring Kate Beckinsale. The song 'Bring Me the Disco King' also features John Frusciante from the Red Hot Chilli Peppers and Maynard James Keenan from Tool.

...

Übermensch

Bowie held a fascination with philosopher Friedrich Nietzsche's concept of the *Übermensch*, meaning 'overhuman' or superman – unfortunately also cited regularly as a major influence on Hitler and the Nazi party. At one point Bowie said, 'I always had a repulsive need to be something more than human. I felt very puny as a human. I thought, Fuck that. I want to be a superhuman.' The concept first made an appearance with Ziggy Stardust, but was most prevalent throughout *Station to Station*.

...

UFOs

Bowie claimed that as a child in England he had seen many unexplained objects in the sky. He said, 'They came over so regularly we could time them. Sometimes they stood still, other times they moved so fast it was hard to keep a steady eye on them.'

HAPPY BIRTHDAY OLD CHAP!

Bowie sent Underwood a hamper every year for his birthday.

After Bowie's death Underwood said, 'I am in shock. I didn't believe it at first. I thought it was some kind of joke but it is for real. My best friend has died.'

Bowie later said of Underwood's paintings, 'George has, over the years, refined his work to the point where I would put him among the top figurative painters coming out of the UK right now.'

Bowie and Underwood were in a band together in high-school called George and the Dragons. Afterwards Underwood played guitar in some of Bowie's bands – The Hooker Brothers, The King Bees and The Konrads.

Underwood designed the sleeve art for Bowie's *Hunky Dory* and *The Rise and Fall of Ziggy Stardust and the Spiders from Mars* as well as album artwork for Mott the Hoople and Tyrannosaurus Rex (T. Rex), among others.

Underwood painted many pictures of Bowie including one called, 'Snow White Tan'.

DAVIE JONES with THE KING BEES

Bowie and Underwood made a record as The King Bees. This was after the fight, so it was clear that they remained friends.

U is for

UNDERWOOD

Richard George Underwood was Bowie's best friend at school. He was also famously responsible for Bowie's mismatched eyes. At the age of 15, in a fight over a girl (Bowie was a bit of a brawler when he was younger, despite his waif-like frame), Underwood hit Bowie in the left eye, accidentally scratching his retina with a fingernail and paralysing the muscle that relaxes and contracts the pupil. The condition, anisocoria, stayed with Bowie throughout his life. And so did George Underwood, as it happened. They remained firm friends, and Underwood went on to become an artist and graphic designer, specialising in book covers and album artwork.

V is for VISCONTI

Tony Visconti is an American record producer who worked regularly with Bowie across the breadth of his career, from their first meeting in 1969 right up to Bowie's final album, *Blackstar*. The two were life-long friends, and Visconti recently recounted at SXSW that he initially hated *Space Oddity* and passed on producing it at the time, 'Then David comes back to me and says, "Well, we got that out of the way. Let's get on with the album".' Visconti was shocked Bowie still wanted to work with him, 'We went on and made that album [*The Man Who Sold the World*]. I still didn't quite know what I was doing, but it's considered a classic.' Visconti was particularly instrumental in Bowie's famous Berlin Trilogy of *Low*, *Heroes* and *Lodger*. He frequently played the bass guitar on Bowie's albums, and often performed live with him as well – he was even the bass guitarist in the Bowie/Mick Ronson side-project, The Hype. He is also known for helping propel Marc Bolan to super-stardom with his album *Electric Warrior*, and for arranging the strings on the Paul McCartney and Wings album *Band on the Run*.

While recording *Blackstar* Visconti noted the lyrics. He said he thought at the time, 'You canny bastard, you're writing a farewell album.'

A week before his death, Bowie told Visconti that he wanted to make one more album.

Visconti once recalled his time in New York with Bowie and John Lennon, 'We did mountains of cocaine, it looked like the Matterhorn, obscenely big, and four open bottles of cognac,' saying that Bowie was 'taking so much it would have killed a horse'.

Visconti is married to May Pang, John Lennon's former lover.

Visconti was one of the few people to know about Bowie's illness. Bowie turned up to a recording session after chemotherapy. Visconti said to *Rolling Stone*, 'He had no eyebrows and he had no hair on his head. There was no way he could keep it a secret from the band. But he told me privately and I got really choked up when we sat face to face talking about it.'

V
is also for

V&A
The Victoria and Albert Museum in London is responsible for the hugely popular *Bowie Is* exhibition that now tours the world. The museum proudly counts the stunning *Diamond Dogs* stage set as well as many of his most famous costumes in their collection.

...

Vampires
Bowie plays a vampire in the 1983 Tony Scott film *The Hunger*. While the 'sexy vampire' trope is a perfect fit for Bowie, they bucked convention and instead used the film to present the portrait of a withering, decaying man, somewhere between living and dying. Bowie obsessive Peter Murphy from proto-goth band Bahaus appears at the start of the movie in a cage singing his ode to the original movie Dracula 'Bella Lugosi's Dead'.

...

'Velvet Goldmine'
A song originally intended for *Ziggy Stardust* but didn't make the final album cut due to risqué lyrics ('let my seed wash your face', anyone?). The song was originally called 'He's a Goldmine', and was written from the viewpoint of a fan singing to Ziggy. It was instead used as the B-side for the '75 re-issue of *Space Oddity*. The song title was used by Todd Haynes for his glam rock-era film starring Jonathan Rhys Myers as a thinly-veiled version of Bowie.

...

'V-2 Schneider'
This mostly instrumental track from *Heroes* was an ode to Florian Schneider from Kraftwerk. Bowie was obsessed with the group during his Berlin period. The 'V-2' refers to the first ballistic missile, the American V-2 rocket but it's unclear why Bowie put the two ideas together in the title. The track was the B-side to the single release of 'Heroes' in 1977.

is also for

Andy Warhol

Andy was a great influence for Bowie. He recorded the song "Andy Warhol" for the album Hunky Dory. Warhol hated it but they bonded over some shoes that Bowie was wearing that Andy took a liking to. Bowie portrayed Andy Warhol in the Jean-Michel Basquiat biopic.

...

'Wild is the Wind'

Written by Dimitri Tiomkin and Ned Washington for the film of the same name, 'Wild is the Wind' was covered twice by Nina Simone. As Bowie was a big fan, he decided to record his lush and melancholy take for *Station to Station*. Like 'Sorrow' before it, his version was so good that the song has always been identified with him, despite being a cover.

...

White Witch

Cherry Vanilla, Bowie's publicist in the 70s, said that at a time when Bowie's cocaine use had rendered him paranoid and obsessed with the occult, he requested Cherry procure white witch Walli Elmlark – a spiritualist who had recorded the album *The Cosmic Children* with Robert Fripp – to perform an exorcism of his LA home. According to Angie, they had performed a ritual which had made the swimming pool bubble and led to the appearance of a dark shadow at the bottom of the pool, which Bowie thought was the mark of the devil.

...

'Walk on the Wild Side'

Bowie and Mick Ronson produced this classic and infamous track from Lou Reed's *Transformer*. Reed Ross, who had lived near Bowie in England and had tutored a young Bowie in saxophone, played the sax solo on the track.

Bowie wears a T-shirt in the video, which says 'Song of Norway'. This is believed to be a reference to his former lover Hermione Farthingale, who left Bowie to take a role in the stage musical *Song of Norway* in Denmark.

The video features Bowie and a girl now known to be director Tony Oursler's wife, artist Jacqueline Humphries. Bowie picked her because she bore a resemblance to Coco Schwab, Bowie's manager (and suspected lover) during the Berlin years, who had helped Bowie kick his cocaine addiction.

The video features an array of places in Berlin, including the auto-repair shop below the apartment in which Bowie lived. It also features an unusual collection of objects, mannequins, bottles, an eyeball, eggs, a snowflake, a giant blue ear and a crystal, all thought to be items that Bowie may have had in his Berlin apartment.

W is for WHERE ARE WE NOW?

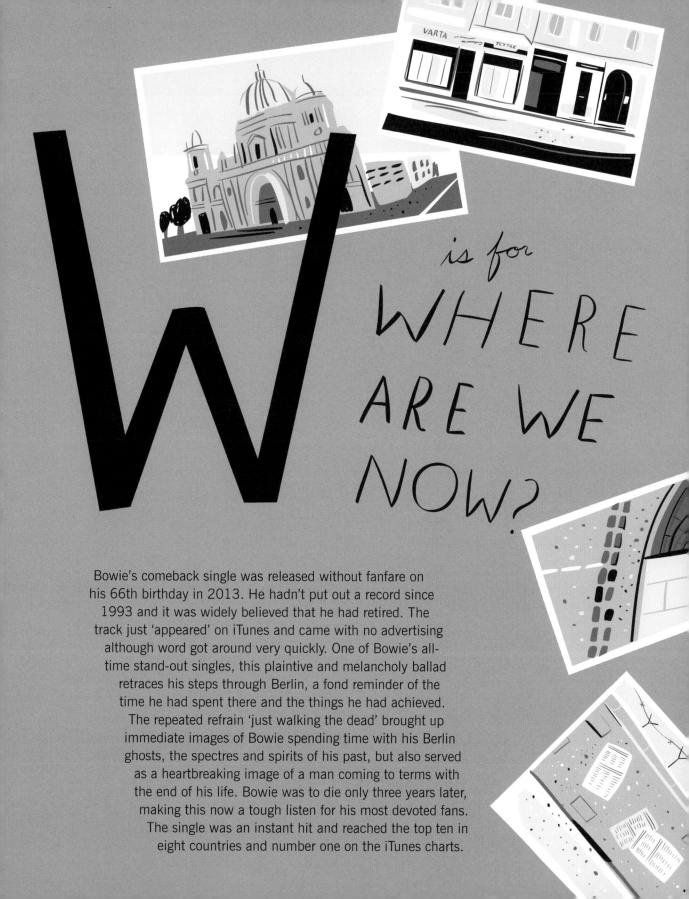

Bowie's comeback single was released without fanfare on his 66th birthday in 2013. He hadn't put out a record since 1993 and it was widely believed that he had retired. The track just 'appeared' on iTunes and came with no advertising although word got around very quickly. One of Bowie's all-time stand-out singles, this plaintive and melancholy ballad retraces his steps through Berlin, a fond reminder of the time he had spent there and the things he had achieved. The repeated refrain 'just walking the dead' brought up immediate images of Bowie spending time with his Berlin ghosts, the spectres and spirits of his past, but also served as a heartbreaking image of a man coming to terms with the end of his life. Bowie was to die only three years later, making this now a tough listen for his most devoted fans. The single was an instant hit and reached the top ten in eight countries and number one on the iTunes charts.

is for X **RATED**

Bowie's first foray into 'adult' territory was in 1967 when he starred in a 14-minute horror film called *The Image*. He played a portrait that comes to 'life' as a ghost and goes on a killing spree. It holds the distinction of becoming the first short film to get an X rating due to its graphic nature. From full frontal nudity in *The Man Who Fell to Earth*, cavorting naked on the beach with Geeling Ng in the 'China Girl' video, snogging and feeling up Catherine Deneuve in the shower in *The Hunger* or playing bondage games with Rosanna Arquette in *The Linguini Incident*, Bowie was definitely no prude when it came to 'adult themes' on screen.

According to 70s groupie Lori Mattix, she was 15 when she was 'de-virginised' by Bowie. Mattix recalled to *Thrillist* recently, 'He walked me through his bedroom and into the bathroom, where he dropped his kimono. He got into the tub, already filled with water, and asked me to wash him. Of course I did. Then he escorted me into the bedroom, gently took off my clothes, and de-virginised me.' The age of consent at the time in California was 18 making this an incidence of statutory rape, but Mattix looks back on the incident fondly, saying, 'Who wouldn't want to lose their virginity to David Bowie?'

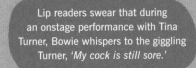

Lip readers swear that during an onstage performance with Tina Turner, Bowie whispers to the giggling Turner, *My cock is still sore.*

According to rumour, Bowie had in his London lounge room a four foot-deep fur-covered bed for orgies, nick-named 'the pit'.

In a 1996 interview Bowie said, 'I have done just about everything that it is possible to do.'

Angie said that the night before their wedding, she and Bowie had dinner at a friend's, which ended up in 'plenty of lively sex'. As a result, they only just arrived at the wedding on time.

X

is also for

Xylophone

Bowie played xylophone on the instrumental 'Weeping Wall' from 1977's *Low*. He also played guitar, vibraphone, synthesisers and piano.

...

Xerox machine

In 1974, Alice Cooper and rock biographer Steve Gaines visited Bowie at the St Regis Hotel in New York. Bowie had rented a colour Xerox machine. Gaines recounts how Bowie asked him if he wanted his portrait taken. He said yes, and Bowie held his head onto the Xerox machine and told him to keep his eyes open. It was reported that at the time Bowie made anyone who came into the hotel have their Xerox portrait taken, always with their eyes open. Bowie later described himself as 'a human Xerox machine'.

...

The X Factor

In 2013, host Simon Cowell said, 'I think if I could have anyone [as a judge] on *The X Factor* it would be David Bowie. It's no secret I've asked him, and he hasn't said yes yet, but I'll keep extending the invitation.'

...

X

While Bowie wrote and recorded a lot of songs, not one of them starts with the letter X.

Y

is also for

The Young Ones
In the ninth episode of British comedy *The Young Ones*, entitled 'Nasty', Rik Mayall recites the lyrics to 'Ashes to Ashes' during a funeral scene. Monty Python's Terry Jones plays the very drunk vicar. When the vicar begins the eulogy with 'Ashes to ashes…' Rik breaks in singing, 'Fun to funky, we know Major Tom's a junkie', before being head-butted by Jones and falling into the open grave. Later in the episode a vampire, played by Alexei Sayle, says, 'You were completely taken in by my phony South African accent.' Neil replies, 'Oh, I thought you were Australian, like David Bowie.'

…

'Yassassin'
A track from Bowie's album *Lodger*, released as a third single in Turkey and Holland. The name is Turkish for 'long life'.

…

Yuletide
Bing Crosby's 21st (and final) Christmas special was filmed in London in 1977. Bowie and Crosby had 45 years between them, and appearing in Yuletide blazers to sing 'The Little Drummer Boy' merged with 'Peace on Earth' seemed a strange concept indeed – but the result is a standout moment in 70s television. Bowie's rapport with Crosby is charming and Crosby's delivery contrasted with Bowie's gentle counterpoint creates quite an emotive experience. Afterwards Crosby asked Bowie for his home number, a great compliment. Sadly Crosby died a month later.

…

Yellowbeard
Bowie has an uncredited cameo in Graham Chapman's 1980 film *Yellowbeard*. He plays 'the shark', or rather, a man with a shark fin on his back.

" I heard the news today OOOH BOY…"

'Fame' features a line from the Beatles' 'A Day In A Life': *I heard the news to day, oh boy!*

Tony Visconti recorded the album in Philadelphia. Bowie wanted it to be as 'live' as possible. Visconti says that at least 80 per cent of the album features direct live recordings with full band set-up – including the vocals.

Bowie brought in then-unknown Luther Vandross to sing backing vocals on the album. Bowie was so impressed he got Vandross to open for some of his shows and pushed him to pursue a solo career. The album also featured Sly and the Family Stone drummer Andy Newmark, as well as Carlos Alomar who would go on to work with Bowie for the next 30 years.

Carlos Alomar came up with the famous neo-funk riff for 'Fame'. He describes how he would lay down the instrumental tracks first, then Bowie would write the lyrics. In a few cases Alomar didn't hear the finished product until the record came out.

Saxophone on the album (including the classic riff on 'Young Americans') was played by David Sanborn, who also played baritone sax on Bruce Springsteen's 'Born to Run'.

Toni Basil of 'Mickey' fame worked as Bowie's choreographer for the *Young Americans* tour.

The song 'Fame' came out of a jam between Bowie, Carlos Alomar and John Lennon, although Bowie wrote all of the lyrics. Lennon sang the word 'aim' over the chorus, which Bowie then changed to 'fame'.

Y is for YOUNG AMERICANS

David Bowie's ninth album, *Young Americans* (and the single of the same name), was a radical and intentional departure for the superstar. Moving away from the fractured Ziggy and Aladdin Sane and all the influences that informed them, Bowie eschewed the invention of a character and instead aimed himself at winning over the American public. He developed a keen interest in Philadelphia soul, gospel and R&B and started working funk and disco beats into his sound. He changed his image as well. Gone was the outrageous excess of costume and glitter that was glam. Instead, Bowie pared back his style and went for a sharper, more tailored look, with suits and hair in a striking array of colours. Bowie referred to his new sound as 'plastic soul'. The gamble paid off. The album reached the top ten and the second single from the album, 'Fame', reached number one on the singles charts in the US.

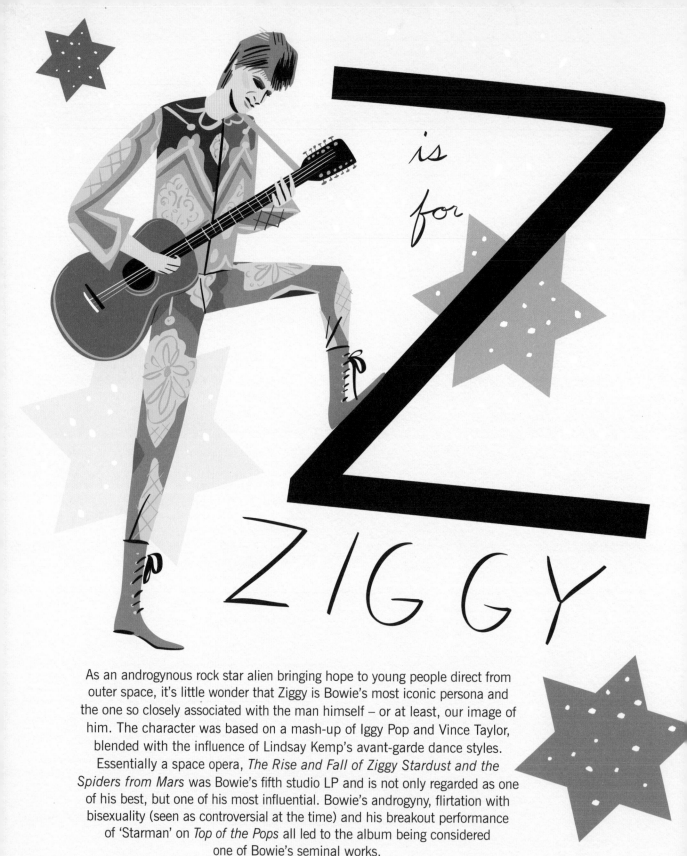

is for

Z

ZIGGY

As an androgynous rock star alien bringing hope to young people direct from outer space, it's little wonder that Ziggy is Bowie's most iconic persona and the one so closely associated with the man himself – or at least, our image of him. The character was based on a mash-up of Iggy Pop and Vince Taylor, blended with the influence of Lindsay Kemp's avant-garde dance styles. Essentially a space opera, _The Rise and Fall of Ziggy Stardust and the Spiders from Mars_ was Bowie's fifth studio LP and is not only regarded as one of his best, but one of his most influential. Bowie's androgyny, flirtation with bisexuality (seen as controversial at the time) and his breakout performance of 'Starman' on _Top of the Pops_ all led to the album being considered one of Bowie's seminal works.

The Spiders from Mars were originally a band called The Rats. Bowie changed the name when he hired them to play on *Hunky Dory*.

When Bowie announced Ziggy's retirement from music on stage, the music press thought that Bowie himself was retiring.

The Spiders from Mars split as Bowie's backing band due to a pay dispute.

In 1987, *Rolling Stone* ranked *Ziggy* as number six of the 100 best albums of the last 20 years.

Bowie launched his *Ziggy Stardust* stage show at the Toby Jug pub in Tolworth in February 1972.

Although the Spiders were reluctant to wear make-up and glitter at first, they relented when they realised that it attracted the girls

In 1996, Bowie said that Ziggy was inspired by Vince Taylor, a failed British rock star who had become obsessed with aliens and Jesus Christ. Taylor gained some popularity in Europe and was known in France as the 'French Elvis'.

The album's popularity, along with Marc Bolan's performance of 'Hot Love' on *Top of the Pops* are seen as catalysts for the glam rock movement.

Z

is also for

Zowie
While at a fairly austere boarding school, Zowie Bowie found that his name drew a lot of attention and ridicule. He changed it to Duncan Jones to avoid this and to 'step out of his father's shadow'. He is now a successful film director.

...

Zigzag
The dramatic Aladdin Sane make-up, sometimes referred to as the lightning bolt, was applied by make-up artist Pierre LaRoche and shot by photographer Brian Duffy. The mark has come to represent the two sides of the character's personality, but Bowie has stated that the inspiration came from a symbol on his oven.

...

Jay-Z
The rapper sampled 'Fame' on his track 'The Blueprint'.

...

Zoo
The Cincinatti zoo named their baby penguin David Bowie just days before Bowie died.

...

'Zion'
This Bowie track was only ever released in bootleg form and is most likely to have been recorded in 1973 at Trident studios as it features Mike Garson on piano, but could also have been recorded during the Pin Up's sessions. Mick Ronson plays guitar and Bowie played the Mellotron – an instrument which was similar to an early sampler. The 'flute' tape loops Bowie used were almost certainly the same ones used by The Beatles for 'Strawberry Fields'. The song was provisionally titled 'Aladdin Vein', 'Love Aladdin Vein', and 'A Lad in Vein', referencing the various provisional titles for *Aladdin Sane*.

Smith Street Books

Published in 2016 by Smith Street Books
Melbourne | Australia
smithstreetbooks.com

ISBN: 978-1-925418-21-7

CIP data is available from the national library of Australia.

Publisher: Paul McNally
Project editor: Hannah Koelmeyer, Tusk studio
Design: Michelle Mackintosh
Illustration: Libby VanderPloeg

Printed & bound in China by C&C Offset Printing Co., Ltd.

Book 20
10 9 8 7 6 5 4 3 2 1

Credits

Cover: inspired by the *Aladdin Sane* album cover, RCA records, 1973. Iconic lightning bolt make-up by Pierre La Roche, photography by Brian Duffy, art direction by Celia Philo. **F is for Fashion:** 'Rites of Spring' black and white vinyl bodysuit designed by Kansai Yamamoto, 1973. **G is for Glam:** white satin suit and red platform sandals designed by Kansai Yamamoto, Space Oddity 'space suit' attributed to Kansai Yamamoto, 1973. **K is for Kemp:** 'Blue Clown' suit designed by Natasha Korniloff for the 'Ashes to Ashes' video, 1980. **L is for Labyrinth:** artwork created in reference to Jareth costume designed by Brian Froud for Jim Henson's *Labyrinth*, a production of Henson Associates, Lucasfilm, The Jim Henson Company, Delphi V Productions and TriStar Pictures. **O is for Oh! You Pretty Things:** artwork created in reference to Brian Ward's *Hunky Dory* cover photo session, 1971. **P is for Pin Ups:** *White Light White Heat* album cover based on 1976 UK cover released by Polydor records. **R is for Rebel Rebel:** artwork created in reference to Gijsbert Hanekroot photos of Bowie as 'Halloween Jack', 1974. **T is for Thin White Duke:** *Station to Station* album art based on 1976 RCA Records release. **U is for Underwood:** 'Davie Jones with the King Bees' album art based on 1964 Decca Vocalion release. **W is for Where Are We Now:** artwork created in reference to Tony Oursler's installation and video for 'Where Are We Now'. **X is for X Rated:** artwork created in reference to the *The Image*, directed by Michael Armstrong, 1969. **Z is for Ziggy Stardust:** Ziggy Stardust quilted two-piece suit designed by Freddie Burretti, 1972. **Imprint page:** artwork created in reference to Mick Rock's video and photographs for 'Life on Mars', 1973. 'Ice-Blue Suit' designed by Freddie Burretti and make-up by Pierre LaRoche.